IN PRAISE OF
MALE CHAUVINISM

IN PRAISE OF
MALE CHAUVINISM

PATRICK SCRIVENOR

DAVID & CHARLES
Newton Abbot   London   North Pomfret (Vt)   Vancouver

ISBN 0 7153 7488 5

Set in 11 on 12pt Aldine Bembo
and printed in Great Britain
by Latimer Trend & Company Ltd Plymouth
for David & Charles (Publishers) Limited
Brunel House Newton Abbot Devon

Published in the United States of America
by David & Charles Inc
North Pomfret Vermont 05053 USA

Published in Canada
by Douglas David & Charles Limited
1875 Welch Street North Vancouver BC

CONTENTS

INTRODUCTION

The terms 'male chauvinism' and 'male chauvinist pig' came into prominence with the growth of the radical feminist movement in the 1960s and 1970s. Like many cant phrases of that era, these terms do not have any clear meaning. The late Nicolas Chauvin, as a result of his passionate attachment to his emperor, lent his name to militant and aggressive patriotism. By tagging 'chauvinism' on to 'male', the feminists were clearly attempting to manufacture an active, implacable foe to act as an excuse for their more extravagant claims and activities. As far as can be discerned, however, the male attitudes that feminists so strongly resent are largely passive, unthinking and automatic, the very reverse of zealous partisanship. In borrowing the pejorative 'pig' from their fellow smart lefties, the feminists clearly indicated where they stood politically—right in the middle of radical chic. The origin of 'pig' is rather obscure. The most interesting suggestion I have heard is that it was culled from George Orwell's *Animal Farm*. If this is so, its use by the left as a term of abuse for representatives of the right is a fascinating distortion of Orwell's portrayal of the pigs in that work.

Since male chauvinism has no clear meaning, it is obvious that in writing in praise of it I can write pretty well what I like, and that is precisely what I intend to do. I'm afraid the lover of serious argument and the seeker after truth will find little to nourish them in these pages, but if, like me, you are constitutionally incapable of taking anything seriously, read on.

I

WOMAN THE TYRANT

or pre-pubescent female dominance in the nuclear family

> Oh what can ail thee, Knight at arms
> Alone and palely loitering . . .

With uncanny prescience Keats gives us the very model of a modern male chauvinist. Tottering feebly about beside some stagnant mere in a condition of wan solitude; the thin shadow of a once-magnificent figure in shining armour, ramping with pennoned lance on his shrill and boastful steed. In the case of Keats' knight it was entirely his own fault. Anyone could have advised him against picking up a girl with long hair and wild eyes who proceeded to practise trick riding in his saddle, sweetly moaning the while. But our modern male chauvinist is not entirely to blame for his plight. Truly 'La belle Dame sans Merci' has got him by the googlies with an unrelenting and taloned fist.

Now, more than ever before, men are awake to their vassal status in women's lives, and this has led them to look back, perhaps seeking a rather false glamour, to ages when men appeared to rule the roost. It is true that male chauvinism reached its finest flowering in earlier days, but throughout all masculine comment on woman's inhumanity to man, in whatever age, there runs a haunting, resigned melancholy.

> Lost is our freedom,
> When we submit to women so:

9

Why do we need them,
When in their best they work our woe?

wrote Thomas Campion, and he should know, having worked for
Elizabeth I, one of the most pronounced and toughest feminists in
the business. (He also wrote the line 'There is a garden in her face'.
Bitterness will out.) Even, therefore, in the days of the most ob-
durate masculine ascendancy, men felt at a disadvantage with
women, and have often gone in fear of them, banding protectively
together in all-male groups. To find out why, we must trace the
development of our male chauvinist from birth.

A male chauvinist is made, not born. No gene leaps ahead at
conception to claim the brat-yet-unformed as a male chauvinist. He
is conditioned by society: the society, so far as his early years are
concerned, of women. The feminists (hereinafter to be called
'femmies') see the male chauvinist as a natural animal: instinctively
arrogant, acquisitive and aggressive. They lavish thousands of
words on the disabilities of their own upbringing and status. Men,
in their view, are just like that.

We must lavish a few words on men's upbringing. At once
distortions in the femmy viewpoint appear in sharp relief. Man was
born free, so why is he everywhere in a low-profile defensive
posture?

Sweet is revenge—especially to women.

Lord Byron, you said a mouthful. Indeed it is, and on that principle
nurseries have been conducted with such thoroughness that scarcely
a male child reaches maturity without feeling outnumbered, out-
gunned, low on rations and almost out of ammunition. His cour-
ageous persistence in these adverse circumstances is deliberately
misrepresented as rudeness, brutality, violence and greed. History is

on the side of the big—well, battalions is as good a euphemism as any.

In the nursery our infant male is wholly subject to feminine sway. The robust among us can cope, and it is the sensitive mind that suffers most from pre-Oedipal mother attachment, as the psychologists so deftly put it. When Oscar Wilde wrote:

All women become like their mothers. That is their tragedy. No man does. That's his.

(a plainly unhinged comment) he was doing more than turning a neat epigram. The echoes of the nursery are almost painfully audible. 'Be a good boy and you'll grow up like mummy.' But he wasn't and didn't. Or did he? Either way the message is clear—it was all his mother's fault.

Even much less sensitive minds are thrown into confusion by over-rigorous potty training. Alfred Lord Tennyson, normally a male chauvinist without a stain on his record, was guilty of lapses that showed how deeply his early conditioning had bitten. Here he is at his best, armed, caparisoned, glittering lance at the ready, socking it to the femmies, and generally telling them where they get off.

Man for the field and woman for the hearth:
Man for the sword and for the needle she:
Man with the head and woman with the heart:
Man to command and woman to obey;
All else confusion.

Impeccable male chauvinist sentiments. But here he is yelping hysterically at the memory of the nappies and the smackings:

Her court was pure; her life serene;
God gave her peace; her land reposed;

A thousand claims to reverence closed
In her as Mother, Wife and Queen.

He was of course referring to Queen Victoria, and the notion that he was discussing the blood royal may have gone to his head. None the less the passage is most significant. Look at the power of the figure evoked in the last line. Mother, Wife, and Queen, all in one and all in capital letters. Pure, serene, peace, repose—all images of the lap, that cosy ledge between overhanging bosom and strong knees where he was wiped, powdered, tickled and generally *handled*—as if he were a household implement. Comfortable memories you will say, but don't miss the note of menace in the use of 'claims' and 'closed'—the parlance of moneylending; but is he describing a mere moneylender? Claims to what? Reverence! This is a holy figure! The great nanny in the skies.

And Queen Victoria does, in a strange way, illustrate the power and subtlety of female dominance—better even than more thoroughgoing femmy cult-heroines like Catherine the Great, Boadicea or the Dagenham Girl Pipers. She was that very subtle femmy variant, the defensive femmy. There can be no doubt that she would have applauded the sentiments of the first extract from Lord Tennyson. Her sickening attitude to superkraut Albert set the tone for more than half a century's husbandly condescension to the little woman. Yet she herself wasn't having any. Her own behaviour as mother, aunt and grandmother would certainly have put the stoppers on any burgeoning Tennyson in the family, and must have contributed to the fact that so many of Europe's crowned heads at the beginning of this century seem to have been either perfectly void or precariously balanced. She did, indeed, become the great nanny in the skies to a huge empire, and found it very, very annoying not to have her own way. She spent a large part of her life half-condescending to a large and romantic-looking highlander (surely a most potent symbol of *machismo*) who habitually wore a kilt. Work it out yourself.

A mother figure indeed, and a powerful one. Look how well her children behaved. Neatly and respectably dressed, they annexed a sizeable chunk of the world's natural resources, used them, sold the resultant products, invested the gain, fathered large families for their own mini-Vickies to rule over, and all with a nervous eye over one shoulder hoping to win a gleam of approval from a very small widow getting on in years. So many aggressive masculine undertakings on behalf of a woman who *herself* had gone out of her way to personify wifely duty. The enigma of female domination in a nutshell.

Not all men are as crippled by mother thralldom as the Victorians were, and even they had the suspicion that perhaps they were unlucky.

> When the coster's finished jumping on his mother

is clearly an agonised *crie de coeur* by a member of the middle class terrified that in some natural, exuberant, uninhibited way the proletariat have got something that he hasn't. Poor Gilbert died before D. H. Lawrence shouted the good news—the working classes, too, live in mother thralldom.

The publication of *Sons and Lovers* in 1913, containing the most minutely described mother fixation outside Sigmund Freud's unreadable notebooks, cannot entirely be cleared of blame in the events of a year later. Historians must lament that Sociology was unheard of in 1914, with the tragic result that no one was at hand to record the confused and pathetic utterances of a whole generation who, with their clear young perception sharpened by Lawrence's seminal prose, flocked to the colours, not in defence of Empire, or even Belgium, but to escape their mothers. What a chance was there lost for the historian of male chauvinism 'Post-Oedipal Matriarchy and the Escalation of Global Conflict.' The campus libraries of the world are poorer places for such a lack.

But while the highbrows give the game away directly, by agonising about their mothers, the writers of popular fiction indicate no less clearly the domination of men by women through a very curious reticence. *Very few of the tough, masculine heroes have mothers.* This is not a device to suggest that they are in some way supernatural. Most authors make it clear that nature has taken its course. Somewhere we surmise (surely never in Baker Street), Mr and Mrs Holmes Senior have lowered themselves to the level of the beasts of the field and the infant Sherlock has been given life, but we are never introduced to them. (A philoprogenitive couple this, since Mycroft was born of earlier two-backed-beastliness.) What of Mrs Hannay, Mrs Drummond, Mrs Biggles, Mrs Dan Dare, Mrs Bond? It is part of the appeal of such heroes that they are free of mother thralldom. (A fascinating and sophisticated departure from the 'no mother' rule was provided by a television programme about a putative secret service outfit whose chief was called 'Mother', played by a very fat actor, always to be found sitting down engaged in long telephone conversations.) Don Quixote, Casanova, Spider-man, Bertie Wooster, Bristow—all these dazzling exemplars of machismo present themselves before us as essentially motherless figures.

And, for the most part, sisterless too. As the young male chauvinist progresses, mother domination is augmented by sister harassment. Little insight is needed to divine that the sentiment

> For there is no friend like a sister
> In calm or stormy weather;
> To cheer one on the tedious way,

To fetch one if one goes astray,
To lift one if one totters down,
To strengthen whilst one stands.

was penned by a woman, Christina Rossetti. Insufferable cow! The mental somersault by which she contrives to list all a sister's vices as if they were virtues underlines the central evil of sisterdom—*always being in the right*. Small wonder that both Christina's brothers were forced to flee into a rather bogus brotherhood (clearly an attempt to escape from the hideous, soupy femininity depicted above) and that one even sank to the depths of working for the Inland Revenue.

Christina's picture of herself as a sister needs examination from a brother's point of view. To start with, her claims are patently exaggerated. Whoever heard of a sister going out in stormy weather? She would certainly grass on her brother had he illicitly gone out in the rain, but go out herself? Never. Then, just as he has reached the desired state of anaesthesia to endure the ennui of a family outing, what does she do? Reminds him of his tedious whereabouts; reminds others of his presence; and generally stirs things to an intolerable level of activity—all in the name of being sweet, bright and sociable. Later in life, when the brother hopes to slope off for a quick under-age drink at the local, she rushes off (bold hussy) and fetches him back. If the brother is lucky enough to get a really gratifying ration of grog under his belt before she shows up, what then? She ostentatiously holds him up, even to the extent of supporting him when he is perfectly vertical. Fifteen or sixteen years of this sort of thing leave their mark.

It is a mark that lasts. In *Macbeth* Shakespeare does not give us the weird aunts, or the weird mothers-in-law. The witches are sisters. Cackling over their pot (sisterly cuisine is a separate and vast subject, but this could be a starting point), making irritatingly obscure but definite pronouncements, and then cackling again in an 'I told you so' manner when some poor sod following their advice lands up to his neck in the cocky-leeky—a perfect picture of sisterdom.

It is the essence of sisterdom to confuse. By the time sisters begin to make their impact, the young male chauvinist has adjusted himself to the fact that women are dominant. The basic brain-washing is over. Now the sister must begin to demonstrate the enormous scope and subtlety of this dominance. Straightforward submission will never do. There are times when the male must seem to be in command—particularly in prohibited enterprises that might carry a penalty. The male must be goaded into a token demonstration of his greater physical strength, not only to put him in the wrong over whatever matter is at hand, but, more importantly, to teach him that women, though often smaller, can always conjure up retribution out of nowhere. The young male learns to accept sudden and arbitrary female justice, rather as the Old Testament Jews learnt to accept the thunderbolts of their irascible God.

It is no surprise to find in the Old Testament the earliest example of sister-induced disorientation. The 'Song of Songs' is an out-pouring of magnificent ambivalence. The first person is lost in time, totally lost geographically, and even hovers between the two sexes. Clutching wildly at any simile to fit his line, he tells his love that her hair is like a flock of goats, and then, getting wilder and wilder

Your cheeks are like halves of a pomegranate behind your veil.
Your neck is like the tower of David, built for an arsenal.

Then, unable to identify this goaty fruit stuck on top of a Martello tower, he makes a wild guess, welling straight up from the sibling rivalry identity psychosis of his youth:

> You have ravished my heart, my sister, my bride.

Having hit off this, to him, plausible explanation (sorry, synthesis) of his turbulent feelings, he is unable to let it alone and returns to it over and again. Thousands of years separate the Old Testament and *Portnoy's Complaint*, but the children of Israel are still afflicted by the same old problem—their women.

Almost every work of femmy propaganda contains some reference to castration. In some cases it is merely a polite nod in the direction of Freud's ludicrous contention that small children are able to grasp the idea that they have been castrated (girls) or may at any moment be castrated (boys). Sometimes the theme forms the title and main argument of a book, as in Germaine Greer's *The Female Eunuch*. Quite why this notion preys with such intensity on the femmy consciousness is not clear. Obviously it is impossible, literally, to castrate a woman. What they seem to mean by this ridiculously inflated metaphor is that their upbringing is organised to rob them of some wonderful, outgoing, dynamic quality which is by this means purloined for the exclusive benefit of men. A very characteristic sisterly argument—'*He* did it!'.

I would not go so far as to suggest that the pattern of mother thralldom and sister harassment is designed to castrate, literally or metaphorically, the young male chauvinist. As subsequent chapters will reveal, his services in this respect are needed to complete his subjection to women. At this point it is sufficient to note that, in childhood, women establish a sway over men that is never properly broken.

> I know I have the body of a weak and feeble woman, but I have the heart and stomach of a king, and of a king of England too; and think

foul scorn that Parma or Spain, or any prince of Europe, should dare to invade the borders of my realm.

So spake Elizabeth to her troops at Tilbury. Translated from feminese it reads:

There don't seem to be very many of you. The best trained, best equipped, largest and most experienced army in the world is about to invade this country, something that I intensely resent. However, being a woman, I don't have to do anything about it. You, on the other hand, do . . .

She didn't need to say any more. They got the message. But notice the underhand appeal to their protective masculine reflexes (conditioned, of course, during their period of mother thralldom) swiftly followed by a reminder of who she is, with the implied reminder of what might happen if any of them didn't feel frightfully like fighting that day. Whatever misfortunes may have befallen the femmies of the twentieth century, no one had castrated Elizabeth Tudor. She was all balls.

The passage illustrates admirably how easily the mother figure is able to continue to exert her dominance over the male long after he has left the home, and even over a fairly 'liberated' male caste, the brutal and licentious soldiery.

As the young male chauvinist approaches sexual maturity, his feelings towards women become entirely antagonistic. He has learnt the hard way that they always win; that, compared with them, he is hopelessly slow-witted and shackled by considerations of honour and fairness to which no woman gives a second thought. His mother has shown him that women must be obeyed. His sister has shown that if he obeys her he invariably gets into trouble. He has been deliberately shielded from any knowledge of his future role in the woman's world—just to make the shock the greater.

However, desperate though his plight appears, this is the watershed of the male chauvinist's development. He is outgrowing women in size, so that at least he has physical strength on his side. More importantly, he is entering the years of sexual initiation, and it is in these years that his only hope of escaping permanent subjection lies. Rather as an army must sometimes expose its flanks to complete some advantageous manoeuvre, so must women, in order to complete man's subjection, expose what is at once their greatest strength and greatest weakness. Handled correctly, this weakness may give the young male the confidence to break through to the broad sunlit uplands of arrogance, selfishness, condescension and lust—the happy grazing grounds of the fully fledged male chauvinist. Many never break through at all. Still more break through to a sort of half-way point where they are capable of intermittent bursts of independence, but are always liable to slide back.

Such a one was Rudyard Kipling. Capable, at his best, of writing lines of such dismissive condescension that, even today, they still drive femmies to the uttermost extremes of fury, his own home life was dominated by his tiresome American wife, and, doubtless under her influence, he could descend into the state of gibbering whimsy exemplified in the lines

> Father, mother and me
> Sister and Auntie say
> All the people like us are We,
> And every one else is They.

That's where they want you. In a tight little matriarchal group where their dominance is most easily exercised. Even those who do break through to full male chauvinism still bear the scars dealt out to them in childhood. Let us then follow our scarred young male into the next round of his fight with women—the only round in the whole fight in which the odds are even. But as he tiptoes nervously into the sexual arena, a pale gleam of light streaks the horizon. If the femmies have their way, the match may be indefinitely postponed. In the graceful, limpid prose that characterises femmy writing, 'We must destroy the institution of heterosexual sex which is a manifestation of the male-female role.' (Manifesto of The Feminists, a rabidly zealous group of New York femmies dedicated to something they call the 'function-activity theory'. Search me.)

So where is this institution? Can we all join, or is there a waiting list? And what of our emergent male chauvinist? Come, let us enrol him before abolition arrives.

2

WOMAN ON HER BACK
or the inverted sex role power syndrome

It was at my Lord Chesterfield's that a lady approached the doctor, and, hoping to confound him, asked: 'Pray tell me, Doctor, wherein lies the difference between a man and a woman?' The doctor did not immediately reply, being engaged in peeling an orange, but at length he observed with much drollery: 'Madam, I cannot conceive.'

(This anecdote may have come from Boswell's *Life of Johnson*. It is just as likely that Sydney Smith was its originator, or Oscar Wilde, or Maurice Bowra, or any of the great jokesmiths. But in attributing the remark to Johnson I have achieved what the art and literary critics call a 'psychological truth': that is, a falsehood, but one which corresponds with the preconceptions of both the liar and the lied-to.)

Rape, then, is an effective political device.
Barbara Mehrhof and Pamela Kearon: *Rape, An Act of Terror.*

This is neither true nor false. Nor is it even a teeny weeny psychological truth. It is what we in the anti-femmy business call MT, or meaningless tripe. It is a very typical femmy utterance, seeking to suggest the existence of a huge conspiracy behind a random, if common, crime.

These two quotations go straight to the heart of the sex-power problem; a problem over which the femmies cudgel their brains till one fears for their sanity. It is a problem that can be stated quite simply: men cannot conceive children; and women, except in rather lurid circumstances with which we need not concern ourselves, cannot commit rape. This the femmies find infuriating. The very thing that is unique to them as women, the bearing of children, is the one factor in their lives that limits their freedom of movement and gives the male a brief opportunity to escape their dominance. The one thing that is unique to men, it is impossible for women to visit upon men in retaliation—much as they would like to.

Good Lord, I hear the reader protest, surely sex is fun? What is this fuss about?

> What is it men in women do require?
> The lineaments of gratified desire.
> What is it women do in men require?
> The lineaments of gratified desire.

This charming picture of mutual satiety may be all right for you and me, and even for William Blake. But, bless his little *Songs of Innocence*, that's not what it's like in the real world, where the femmies live. *Sex is political.*

Sex is the one area in which women find their accustomed superiority to men reduced to near parity. Therefore everything about sex that they find to their disadvantage is ascribed to a male conspiracy. It was, of course, a committee of male chauvinists that designed their mammary appendages, so endearing to the admirer, such an encumbrance to the wearer. The tendency of men to reach satisfaction faster than women is a plot to deny women the full pleasures of sex. Even the fact that most couples, however various and athletic the alternatives they try, collapse at some point along the path to ecstasy into what, in deference to a thousand saloon-bar humorists, I must call the missionary position—even this is taken as symbolic of a concerted male attempt to put women at a disadvantage. It is clear that they *feel* at a disadvantage in sexual matters, and on to this the budding male chauvinist must batten.

When the emergent male encounters his first extra-familial woman he has to adjust to a series of shocks. The idea that she might want something beyond a combined punch-bag and domestic servant is new to him. He may, with infantile precosity, have previously made attempts on his sister or some other female member of the family. These advances will not have been received in a way to prepare him for the fact that this new woman is here to be screwed, and may even want to be screwed. The woman, on the other hand, will have a very clear idea of what she wants, and she will use all her skill to ensure that in getting it she does not allow the young male to rise above his basic slave/punch-bag status. He, driven by the raging taskmaster, may be blinded by the imminence of oats to this central fact: whether or not the two hit the pit together is not the point at issue. Nowadays they almost certainly will. It is on what terms they hit the pit that counts. The terms are very rarely stated (or, in femmy parlance, the central dialectic remains unarticulated), but in a myriad of small ways the woman can manoeuvre the man into attitudes of obligation, guilt, doubt, savage rut, even love—all of which will serve to keep him in a properly servile condition. It is the male chauvinist's job to avoid all these pitfalls.

This question of who ends up on top makes the early sex life of the young male—beneath the pleasure and the excitement of finding that not all women are mothers, sisters or aunts—a savage battlefield. And women conduct the battle with particular ferocity.

Take, for example, *Jane Eyre*. In many respects she is the fictional prototype of a femmy. With great subtlety Charlotte Brontë confronts her with someone who might well be the fictional prototype of a male chauvinist, the Byronic Mr Rochester. For the purposes of the story Rochester is allowed to be fascinating, but his quick temper, his swift, decisive actions, his ruthlessness, all mark him down, from the femmy point of view, as the enemy. Now what does Miss Brontë do? She makes the proud, haughty Rochester fall in love with the governess, in spite of her plainness, because of her ready wit and independent spirit. This is a very powerful piece of feminine wish-fulfillment—to be loved as a personality absolutely irrespective of physical appearance. It is clearly a perverse wish. Imagine how far you'd get by saying to a woman, 'Your mind, temperament and personality dazzle me, and I'm only too willing to ignore the fact that you look like the back of a bus.' Besides, Jane Eyre is only very vaguely described as plain. Plenty of room is left to imagine that she might, for example, have fabulous boobs.

Anyway, here we have the prototype male chauvinist as near as dammit grovelling to the prototype femmy. But so savage is the sexual battle, that Miss Brontë is not content with this victory. Firstly she must reveal the full enormity of Rochester's male arrogance—he is married already. Then, to atone for trying to jump the juicy Jane while in a state of wedded—well, not bliss exactly—he must be reduced to a state of complete helplessness. His end is almost too painful to contemplate. Miss Brontë coolly blinds and cripples him in a fire, and only then is he allowed to lay plain Jane. The pessimistic reader may find reason to speculate that the fire has unmanned him even for this.

This is a femmy view of a desirable outcome to the sexual battle. Such vindictiveness is not to be found on the male side, although brittle and unconvincing attempts at bravado may be discerned.

I must have women. There is nothing unbends the mind like them.

Superficially this may appear to be a male chauvinist speaking. (It is not, incidentally, the late President Kennedy, who complained of headaches if he didn't have women with adequate frequency. The line appears in *The Beggars' Opera*, by John Gay.) The possessive 'have'; 'women' in the plural; the light-hearted and transitory pleasure for which they are wanted: all this points to well developed chauvinism. But wait! Is there not an echo of something familiar? Another observation similarly phrased? Why, yes, of course:

> Depend upon it, Sir, when a man knows he is to be hanged in a fortnight, it concentrates his mind wonderfully.

It is the good doctor again, in person this time. Women are referred to as unbending the mind. That is, straightening it, setting it on the right track, concentrating it, in fact. Similarly, hanging 'concentrates the mind'. It is clear that women and hanging are indissolubly linked in the male subconscious. 'Having' a woman entails the risk of death—or at any rate the living death of female dominance. Every time the male enters a new liaison he runs the risk of entrapment. The sexual battle, most acute in the early years, none the less continues throughout active sexual life. (The purist will argue that John Gay died when Johnson was still only twenty-three and that any connection between the two remarks, subconscious or otherwise, must be purely coincidental. Such a purist has not grasped the concept of psychological truth.)

Aside from the private battle that each male chauvinist must conduct for himself, there are a number of public fallacies, put about by women, which, if allowed to take root in the fertile soil of the young male mind, may do incalculable damage to his prospects of reaching adult male chauvinism. The first of these is that there is someone special—a woman who will turn him on as no one else can.

> Tisn't beauty, so to speak, nor good talk necessarily. It's just IT. Some women'll stay in a man's memory if they once walked down a street.

Rudyard Kipling, letting the side down again. Apart from the fact that this passage may be the source of 'IT' as a coy euphemism for sex appeal, there is little to recommend it. Search your memory. How many women can you remember merely from having seen them *once* walk down a street? For a more balanced view we must return to Dr Johnson.

> Were it not for imagination, Sir, a man would be as happy in the arms of a chambermaid as of a duchess.

The advance of socialism has made duchesses rather easier to come by than chambermaids, but there is no need to put the matter to the test. Just keep the imagination under control, and remember— take care of the numbers and the quality will take care of itself.

A second fallacy is that, incurring as they do the risk of pregnancy, women's emotional reactions to sex are mysteriously deep and complicated, more profound than men's and deserving greater consideration. Radical femmies have abandoned this argument as it relies on evolutionary determinism of a kind they are anxious to jettison because of its implications in other fields. Many women, though, still use this weapon. Firstly, the young male must reject this argument and grasp that he, too, is quite likely to become emotionally involved. Secondly,

> I opened to my beloved; but my beloved had withdrawn himself.

Well, yes. There's always that way, but the avoidance of pregnancy can now be less painfully encompassed. It has indeed been possible for a surprisingly long time to ease the woman's burden of worry, and in this respect, contrary to femmy propaganda, men have shown themselves at their most considerate and sensitive. Who, for instance, could resist the dignified and tasteful blandishments of Mr E. Lambert, manufacturer of surgical goods, who, in 1866, revealed to the public the latest of his

MALTHUSIAN APPLIANCES . . . The Improved Vertical and Reverse Current Syringe . . . A new vertical and reverse current vaginal tube, producing a continual current treble the power of the ordinary tubes used for this purpose, thoroughly cleansing the parts it is applied to. It is to be used with injection of sufficient power to destroy the life properties of the spermatic fluid without injury to the person, and if the instructions are followed it can be used with success and safety.

Nowadays the pill has put an end to the charming scenes conjured up by Mr Lambert's advertisement.

The sexual target on which the femmies expend most ammunition, however, is the act itself. To enjoy it straightforwardly would be a betrayal of the femmy cause. For them the act is fraught with symbolism. In any normal sexual act the female organ engulfs the male. So far so good; no symbolism of male dominance there. But this is usually achieved in the above-mentioned missionary position. Anathema! Anathema! *The woman is underneath.* Nor is 'hands, knees and boomps-a-daisy' much improvement. The woman does not actually have to lie down, but she is still *underneath*, and kneeling too. This has led femmy writers to extol the very limited permutations of bodily union that can be managed with the woman on top. Here, they say, penetration is better, orgasm more easily achieved, and the woman controls the rhythm. The physiology of these claims seems doubtful, but so far as I am concerned, you lovely radical ladies you, this is one sit-in you may conduct indefinitely.

Then there's the orgasm itself, and on this subject the fearless femmies wax devastatingly frank.

Although there are many areas for sexual arousal, there is only one area for sexual climax; that area is the clitoris.

Anna Koedt, Myth of the Vaginal Orgasm

Apparently, quite unbeknown to me, a posse of entrenched male chauvinists led by Freud (not Clement, silly, Sigmund) has spent a large part of the twentieth century propagating the idea that female orgasm is achieved by stimulation within the vagina. I find it difficult to read anything written by or about Freud without drifting off into another, better world, so I cannot claim to be fully conversant with the Freud canon, but it seems to me that Freud said that as full sexual experience replaces adolescent masturbation, the woman's sexual *interest* shifts from her clitoris to her vagina. True or false, it is a small move to make, and a small point to labour over since most women can decide for themselves where it feels best. But Koedt is relentless:

> We must begin to demand that if certain sexual positions now defined as standard are not mutually conducive to orgasm, they no longer be defined as standard.

A wizard with words, this girl. She goes on to insist that men perpetuate the 'myth' because they enjoy 'standard' sex, because they are envious of the clitoris as the female equivalent of the penis, and because they fear becoming sexually expendable if women start to enjoy more direct methods of attaining orgasm.

All this, from Freud to Koedt, may be consigned to a large wastepaper container labelled MT. After reading such stuff it is a welcome jolt to remind oneself that most people continue to find the other sex attractive, do something about it, do it again, and again, and again, upside-down, inside-out, here, there, everywhere, without any reference to the femmies and their neurotic worries.

28

Welcome, too, is the demolition of Anna Koedt's argument by Germaine Greer in the terse phrase

Besides, a man is more than a dildo.

Good on yer, Germ, old sport! It's nice to hear the Aussie scourge putting in an unsolicited plug for the one-eyed trouser snake.

What of our nervous young male? We have shown him that the women's order of battle in the sexual line-up has gaps in it—gaps that may be breached and exploited.

> But soon as e'er the beauteous idiot spoke,
> Forth from her coral lips such folly broke,
> Like balm the trickling nonsense heal'd my wound,
> And what her eyes enthralled, her tongue unbound.

Congreve signposts the road out of the trap of sexual thralldom. However potent the spell cast, there is always some aspect of the adored object capable of bringing the adorer up with a nasty jolt. Most women will do their best to conceal this shortcoming. The mindless prattler is one of the easiest to spot. But whenever he finds himself sinking into sexual captivity, the male chauvinist should address himself to seeking out and dwelling on all the little things that displease him. But he shouldn't carry this process too far. Women, after all, are there to be enjoyed.

Perhaps Robert Burns best typifies the zestful carelessness in sex to which the true male chauvinist should aspire, in his description of the young fisherlad and his girl in the hut where he keeps his nets:

> So lay her doun among the creels,
> And jam the door with baith your heels,
> The mair ye bang the mair she squeals,
> And hey for hogmagandie!

Burns' vanity in matters of sexual prowess makes it certain that the squeals referred to are supposed to be squeals of delight, and that the lass in question is a willing partner in hogmagandie. (The title of another verse 'Nine Inch Will Please the Lady' establishes Burns as a male chauvinist of the most highly developed type, if also as something of a braggart.) But what if the Ayrshire of the late eighteenth century had been as awash with femmies as New York is today? The lady's cries would certainly have been overheard and misinterpreted, a rape squad would have surrounded the hut, the pair, hopelessly entangled in the net, would have been dragged from among the creels, and the wretched fisherlad would almost certainly have had all his tackle confiscated, because rape, or forcible hogmagandie, is something the femmies take very, very seriously. And so they should, but, serious or not, it is a subject that drives them to the silliest extremes of their thought, if such it can be called.

> Rape is supported by a concensus of the male class. It is preached by male-controlled and all-pervasive media with only a minimum of disguise and restraint.
>
> Barbara Mehrhof and Pamela Kearon: *Rape: An Act of Terror*

We are all familiar with the enthusiastic sympathy extended by men to the rapists of their wives, girlfriends or daughters, such is the solidarity of the male class, but the role of the media in promoting rape may have slipped by you. Leaders in *The Times*, *The Financial Times* share index, the *Daily Worker*, *The Archers*, *Stars on Sunday*, *Magic Roundabout*, *Upstairs Downstairs*, Pseuds' Corner in *Private Eye*, the *Generation Game*, *Grandstand* (very significant)—all, whatever their ostensible subject, carry the sublimal message: go out and rape, young man.

It is not a message that seems to have much impact, as rape remains very much a minority male interest. It is not of much importance to the male chauvinist, except that he will certainly be attacked, at some point in his life, by a femmy armed with arguments similar to those expressed above. Two countermoves are open to him when this happens. One is to refute vigorously everything she says, categorising it all under the heading of MT. The other is to agree abjectly and adopt a pose of puzzled liberalism heavily dependent on the unspoken implication that 'between us, of course, rape couldn't happen because two such civilised and sensitive people are bound to arrive at mutual consent simultaneously and instantly'. A third course of action is to say nothing at all but to begin to display overt and uncontrollable signs of passion for her—but first make sure she's not armed.

Physically, then, men have a slight advantage in the sexual battle. By brute force and bloody-mindedness they can avoid the shackles of sexual thralldom being added to those of family thralldom. Force and bloody-mindedness will be needed, though. The psychological weapons brought to bear by women during this phase of the battle are powerful indeed.

Outright sexual attraction will be used without any scruple at all. With twitching hands and trembling knees the helpless male will be drawn towards the target. But the wise woman will know that a contrary force is operating—a fear of women bred during the years of oppression. Should custom begin to stale her not-so-infinite variety, this fear may begin to assert itself more strongly than the sex drive, and the young male may begin stepping high and wide for the open spaces of liberty. Here the woman may play upon another male neurosis—the fear of betrayal.

> The fickleness of the women I love is only equalled by the infernal constancy of the women who love me.

Shaw underlines a common plight. Alongside his fear of betrayal, women are able to exploit the young male's sense of obligation. So he finds himself lunging wildly after some creature

31

whose questionable loyalty makes his lunging all the wilder, while clinging to his coat is some other creature whom he is not sufficiently ruthless to shake off. Between them they will certainly cook his goose, and even a single woman, by neatly balancing lust, jealousy and weakness, can achieve easy domination.

We have come a long way from the ability to conceive and the inability to commit rape that lie at the bottom of women's tactics in the sexual battle, but they need restating. Part of women's motives in seeking to dominate men (besides their natural inclination to govern) is to secure themselves against the contingency of pregnancy. At the same time they *want* to become pregnant, since this is something unique to them; something there is no possibility of men's doing better. But, since they cannot commit rape, to become pregnant the co-operation of a man is needed, and soliciting that co-operation exposes women to the risk that the man may realise he is needed and become correspondingly independent. Men can't all be blinded and crippled to reduce them to the desired state of vassalage, so every trick and artifice must be used to conceal from them their one source of power, and to use sex as yet another means of subjugation.

A percentage of males, however, gets through this net, and achieves the idyllic state of mind in which they can say, with Philip Dormer Stanhope, Earl of Chesterfield

A man of sense only trifles with them [women], plays with them, humours and flatters them, as he does with a sprightly forward child; but he neither consults them about, nor trusts them with, serious matters.

Here he is at last. Safe through the long years of mother thralldom; bloody but unbowed from the recent sexual battle; coxcomb and wattles aflame; rustling and shaking his metallic plumage; spurs glistening; strutting aggressively—the fully fledged male chauvinist in all his glory.

3

WOMAN THE NUISANCE
or the persistence ratio as a function of the decibel quotient

Women possess one universal, inexhaustible weapon, equally
effective against the male chauvinist, the half-emancipated man, and
the fully subject male. It is the capacity to make a nuisance of themselves in any circumstances and in an endlessly varied number of
guises.

> O Woman! In our hours of ease,
> Uncertain, coy and hard to please,
> And variable as the shade
> By the light quivering aspen made;
> When pain and anguish wring the brow,
> A ministering angel thou!

The exclamation marks, the capital letters, and the generally
grovelling attitude, all mark down Sir Walter Scott as a bad case
of male subjectivism. Nonetheless he inadvertently gives us a good
example of woman the nuisance. Take first 'hours of ease'. If there's
one thing a woman can't stand, it's to see men at ease. Immediately
she falls back on indecision, fractiousness and petulance. As for the
light quivering aspen—well, in his days at Edinburgh High School
Sir Walter was no doubt flogged with all the regularity of late
eighteenth-century schooling, and any good analyst could identify
the schoolmaster's cane in the quivering aspen. All attempts at ease,

then, will be disrupted by this disagreeable figure flitting about carrying with her distant echoes of chastisement and pain.

Things are little better when misfortune strikes—rather worse, if anything. The woman's first consideration is to get herself into a favourable and sympathetic light, and a terrible Florence Nightingale-ism seizes her. Subconsciously, although superficially an admirer of women on such occasions, the poet in Sir Walter identifies the snag straight away. Pain and anguish rarely wring the *brow*, and a ministering angel is not what the sufferer wants. But the woman is not concerned with the sufferer's wants, and would be most put out if they obtruded between the public and her own private picture of herself as a beautiful, bereft creature drooping tragically over some hapless wretch, while dabbing futilely at his forehead with a hanky. A lengthy terminal illness gives the woman the best opportunity to practise this particular brand of nuisance, but victims from the battlefield are preferred on account of their greater glamour. The man, of course, must not be so inconsiderate as to get killed. There is a limit to the length of time that can be spent drooping over a corpse. No, what is needed is a good 'sub-lethal' wound and surroundings in which the woman can be decorative rather than capable.

Lack of capability is another source of nuisance that women have drawn upon with astonishing profit to themselves. They are, of course, perfectly capable, as the femmies never tire of telling us. In government, medicine, law, teaching, in every profession, except perhaps pugilism, women can do as well as men and often better. Why then this affectation of ineptness? The femmies would have us believe it to be the result of a whole system of conditioning engineered by men to keep women in second place. Far fetched, of course. Think how much easier life would be if your wife *could* mend the car. A much more obvious conclusion is that women affect helpless incapacity in order to make more work for the man, to exhaust his patience and to disrupt his peace of mind.

But what is woman?—only one of Nature's agreeable blunders.

Hannah Cowley taking the little woman motif to disgustingly self-congratulatory lengths. O! Don't mind me, I'm just an agreeable little blunder going about looking for somewhere to make a cock-up of things. Even the stern spirit of George Eliot could admit the folly of women, but she had to add a feminist sting to the tail.

I'm not denying the women are foolish; God Almighty made 'em to match the men.

Indeed he did—in this sphere, to outmatch them. The incompetent little woman ploy is brought to bear most often against the true male chauvinist, hardened against most other feminine wiles. It relies for success on the male chauvinist's impatience with slowness and ham-handedness. With a sufficient display of fumbling uselessness, the male chauvinist can usually be provoked into doing the job for the woman, on her terms, and in his time.

The man is not usually in a position to make any effective counter to the Florence Nightingale brand of nuisance, but the little woman nuisance can be most effectively put down. Once the woman has embarked on uselessness as her means of causing annoyance for the day, she has committed herself. She cannot suddenly become a mechanical and practical genius. Let her, therefore, carry on. Heavy material loss may result, but the victory will be worth it.

I am a sundial, turned the wrong way round.
I cost my foolish mistress fifty pound.

What Belloc does not tell us is that the woman knew perfectly well which way round the beastly thing should go. She merely wished to annoy everyone. Her husband, the gardener, the workman who put it in, and that funny little man from Oxford who keeps writing things, but the attempt backfired on her disastrously. Male chauvinists all, they said not a word, and now there the sundial is, firmly cemented into place the wrong way round.

Any woman who tries the little woman act as a means of annoyance runs the risk of meeting a really high-powered male chauvinist like Lord Chesterfield and adding credence to his dictum:

> Women, then, are only children of a larger growth; they have an entertaining tattle, and sometimes wit; but for solid, reasoning good sense, I never knew in my life one that had it, or who reasoned or acted consequentially for four and twenty hours together.

Pompous, yes; intolerably condescending, yes; but they had it coming to them.

The obverse of the little woman nuisance is the blue-stocking nuisance, and here women go into super-charged overdrive in their efforts to annoy and drive mad. Nothing is more formidable than the blue-stocking, and even the most hardened male chauvinist may find, after prolonged exposure to one, that he is slipping back into thralldom.

> *Counsel:* 'But is the jury to understand, Mr Haddock, that in your opinion the highbrow is necessarily of the feminine gender?'
> *Witness:* 'Of course. It is one of the special diseases of women.'

A. P. Herbert, thou shouldst be living at this hour. England hath need of thee. In recent years the disease has become epidemic, and indeed the whole femmy movement can be viewed as a bad outbreak of blue-stockingism. Femmies are blue-stockings to a man. Sorry, to a person.

Although there were earlier outbreaks, femmy blue-stockingism really began with Mary Wollstonecraft in the late eighteenth

36

century. This lucid and intelligent woman was much vilified in her own time, and deserves to be the figurehead of the femmy movement. In the eyes of modern femmies, however, she has seriously blotted her copybook. To start with she lived a whole century before Sigmund Freud, and was therefore criminally ignorant of such matters as penis envy and castration complexes, to the utter detriment of her thought, and to the detriment of her language too—she wrote with disgraceful fluency and clarity.

Far worse in the eyes of modern femmydom are her political impurities. Gymnastics and Socratic argument were all very well for gels of the middle and upper classes, but prole girls, she advocated, should stick to millinery and plainwork. Modern femmies, who long to merge the eccentric interests of their own movement with the larger concern of International Revolution Inc. find this unforgivable.

She was the forerunner, however, of a whole army of high-powered nuisances, some of whom have been so high powered and such a nuisance that only physically are they distinguishable from our hero, the male chauvinist, and not always then. The original blue-stocking group was concerned mainly with literature, but it is too good a term to be confined, and should be applied to any woman with pronounced intellectual, political, or cultural tastes. Defined thus it is easy to trace the rise of blue-stockingism from its beginnings in the nineteenth century to its boom status in the 1970s. Curiously, the nuisance value of blue-stockingism has declined in inverse proportion to the number of its adherents, but its top practitioners are still the male chauvinist's most formidable adversaries.

No greater nuisance can be imagined than politicians in general, and ministers in particular, and it is no surprise to find woman the blue-stocking nuisance taking to this occupation like a duck to water. The first woman to achieve cabinet rank was one Nina Bang,

Denmark's minister for education from 1924 to 1926. By main force I pass over this woman's name without further comment and proceed to the women who have succeeded in this sphere; who have attained the leadership of a country. Immediately a single striking fact emerges—they are nearly all autocrats. This is not just the historical accident that many of them were hereditary queens in ages when autocracy was more widespread. A high proportion of twentieth-century women rulers have been dictators of one complexion or another.

> In men we various ruling passions find;
> In women, two almost divide the kind;
> Those, only fixed, they first or last obey,
> The love of pleasure and the love of sway.

If Pope had lived later he might have added: when the importance that blue-stockings attach to being earnest has eradicated the love of pleasure, the love of sway expands to fill the space available.

Another deeply significant fact about the femmy blue-stocking is that she is nearly always at the van of the *avant garde*. Things may be changing, and Mrs Thatcher may be the first of a long line of blue-rinse blue-stockings, but up to now such women have not figured largely among successful femmies. The characteristic femmy belongs to the smart left, and is as vulnerable to the occupational diseases of her calling as any of her male counterparts.

> When she inveighed eloquently against the evils of capitalism at drawing room meetings and Fabian conferences she was conscious of a comfortable feeling that the system, with all its inequalities and iniquities, would probably last her time. It is one of the consolations of middle-aged reformers that the good they inculcate must live after them if it is to live at all.

The rich socialist and the priviledged revolutionary we are all

38

acquainted with, but Saki puts his finger with unerring accuracy on their state of mind. It is the same oblivious hypocrisy that might prompt a socialist cabinet minister to occupy a private hospital bed, or send the ministry car to chauffeur his children from the local comprehensive to extra private classes. It is particularly common among blue-stockings in whom the love of pleasure is not entirely dead and who enormously enjoy the perquisites of the high positions to which their natural talents exalt them.

Women's fondness for high-powered nuisance is nowhere more evident than in their attitude to their own deliverers. From its origins in America in 1848, the movement for women's rights spread, and spawned many organisations to campaign for various rights, among them the vote. The group on which the femmy imagination has fastened, however, is Mrs Pankhurst's militant suffragette movement. Such potent cult figures are the members of this group, that recently they became enshrined in that most sacred tabernacle, a television series. It is possible to argue that Pankhurst's tactics delayed the arrival of the vote for women by alienating many potential supporters. She certainly didn't *advance* the date of emancipation. But such considerations are trivial. She was a nuisance. Perhaps the biggest nuisance in British politics of this century, including even the Irish. An unchallengeable position.

There is no effective counter to the blue-stocking. To meet her on her own ground requires intellectual gifts that may be lacking; entails painful homework, possibly even the reading of a book, and is boring. Rampant philistinism provides a measure of cover, as the blue-stocking will probably ignore you, but this cannot be relied on. My advice is, run.

There are several sub-genera of blue-stocking, less formidable and rarely representative of full-blooded femmydom. Only one of these is really dangerous, and that is composed of ladies whose tendency it is to go about doing deliberate good. Their numbers have declined of late, but there was a time when no corner of the globe was safe from these women, all of the most autocratic cast of mind. Often they were missionaries; sometimes dedicated to promoting kindness to animals; the most mischievous kind flourished in the 1930s, and were wedded to the proposition that Josef Stalin could do no wrong. It is easy to distinguish them from the less lethal sub-genera. Their heads are broad at the back to accommodate the poison sacs; the teeth are hollow and sometimes hinged to promote efficient delivery of the venom, and the body is often spotted. They should be scotched on sight.

The remaining sub-genera are comparatively small, and contain the only women with whom the male chauvinist is able to get on— those who have found some gainful employ and succeed in it by their own efforts rather than by the skilled deployment of boob, leg and bum. As early as 1919 the Sex Disqualification (Removal) Act made it illegal to discriminate against women entering the professions. Since then extraordinarily few have taken advantage of this freedom. I turn to a radical publication, which calls itself with wonderful candour the Counter Information Service, and find the following figure: fifty-eight years after the act *only 4 per cent of architects are women*. Shocking. But note this: 8 per cent of barristers, double the proportion, are women. Just what you'd expect, of course; the exact, painstaking profession attracts half the proportion of women attracted by the thoroughly argumentative and contentious one. But why have so few bothered to try? Easy. Don't believe the femmies' guff about social pressures, marriage and the feminine mystique. The fact is that working women are thoroughly able, likeable beings—in other words, they've sacrificed their feminine heritage: they are no longer a nuisance. For most it is too great a sacrifice to make.

There is a tide in the affairs of women
Which, taken at the flood, leads—God knows where.

It led Lord Byron into what one biographer furtively describes as 'criminal relations with his half sister', but he is referring here to female caprice, or what we, in days of greater linguistic refinement, must learn to call the inverse perversity curve exponential. That is, the tendency of women's irrational whims to increase in proportion to the victim's willingness to humour them. Not being a sociologist I am unable to express this phenomenon in graph form for my readers, but I'm sure you can imagine the two ascending lines, zigging and zagging upwards across the scientific little squares, each zig the result of months of perfectly futile questions and wholly subjective answers, each zag a thousand pounds' worth of computer time. I cannot bring you these wonders of social science. But then this modest volume is costing you less than two guineas, and if you're as poor as that you are more likely to be the target of a sociologist than to be his reader.

Poets seem to be particularly awake to female caprice. Robert Bridges laments

All women born are so perverse
No man need boast their love possessing.

Byron, of course, boasted of little else, but then he didn't go to Eton, and was never made poet laureate. Both, however, identify a rich source of feminine nuisance: sudden and unpredictable changes of mind. It is a technique less used now than previously, when a certain deference was demanded in outward dealings with women. Now that emancipation has put an end to courtesy, it is easily dealt with. No woman, depending on a man for a lift, who keeps him waiting because she can't decide what to wear, and comes down to find both him and his car gone, ever does it again, to him or any other man. If you never let a woman get away with wilful changes of mind, she won't make them. But it is easier said than done since caprice is often worked in harness with the little woman act (see above) and the combination may well give the impression of a genuine half-wit who really does need to be indulged.

Woman the nuisance, like the poor, is always with us. No man should be too put out by her since the only complete remedy is to avoid women altogether.

> I may not here omit those two main plagues, and common dotages of human kind, wine and women, which have infatuated and besotted myriads of people. They go commonly together.

Beware! This is not true male chauvinism, but pseudo-chauvinism, or misogyny. Robert Burton, who wrote it, must have been a dull fellow indeed. Much healthier were the Australian troops during the war who shouted at an *ENSA* concert party 'WINE, WOMEN AND SONG! AND NOT SO MUCH OF THE BLOODY SINGING!' No, woman the nuisance, in all her guises, is here to stay, and we might as well accept her philosophically. After all,

> There's some diversion in a talking blockhead; and since a woman must wear chains, I would have the pleasure of hearing 'em rattle a little.
> *The Beaux's Stratagem*, George Farquhar

(A disproportionate number of the eligible male chauvinists are either Scotsmen or members of the aristocracy. Is it that Scotsmen are nature's aristocrats, or are aristocrats unnatural Scotsmen?)

So, turn woman the nuisance to your advantage. Let her schemes rebound on her, but, particularly where woman the blue-stocking is concerned, *don't argue*. Remember, as the good book says,

> A continual dropping in a very rainy day and a contentious woman are alike.

Both wear you out.

4

WOMAN THE WIFE
or male abjectivism and the fly-trap analogue

... that pervading influence which sanctifies while it enhances the—a—
I would say, in short, by the influence of Woman, in the lofty character of Wife ...

Perhaps it is rather base to drag Mr Micawber into this squabble
between mere mortals. It would be kinder to leave his delighted
spirit to bathe in fiery floods or to reside in thrilling regions of
thick-ribbed ice, or even to be imprisoned in the viewless winds and
blow with restless violence round about the pendant world, never
losing sight of the fact that at any moment something might turn
up. Mr Micawber stands alone, and perhaps I should not use him.

But use him I must, because nowhere does he stand more alone
than in his opinion of the lofty character of Wife. History and
literature record an almost universal thumbs down to matrimony.
No one, from the most rabid femmy to the most dominating and
acquisitive male chauvinist, can find much to say in favour of
wedded bliss. A scattering of Victorians and sentimental novelists,
plainly in the grip of an extreme form of mother thralldom, put up
a feeble defence, but from all other quarters nothing is heard except
a loud blowing of raspberries.

A subject that finds common ground for Lord Chesterfield and
Germaine Greer must indeed be worth examining.

It is so far from being natural for a man and woman to live in a state of marriage that we find all the motives which they have for remaining in that connection, and the restraints which civilised society imposes to prevent separation, are hardly sufficient to keep them together.

The restraints that Dr Johnson mentions have been lifted, or at any rate considerably relaxed, but matrimony is still committed among an astonishingly high proportion of the population. When young people embarking on life so often choose to do so together, what happens to produce the widespread contempt in which the holy estate is held? The femmies blame male chauvinism, male selfishness, and the horrors of housework. Men blame the intolerably erratic nature of female behaviour, the cost of having to support a family, and the rapidity with which their wives age. Of both these views, more later.

In matters of religion and matrimony I never give any advice; because I will not have anybody's torments in this world or the next laid to my charge.

Philip Dormer Stanhope, Earl of Chesterfield

(I'm getting fed up with this guy. He's too ponderous by half. Let us, therefore, put the skids under him. In Johnson's words, 'This man I thought had been a Lord among wits; but, I find, he is only a wit among Lords.' This is the last we shall hear from our witty lord.)

However, in mentioning religion he may have hit the nub. It is the Prayer Book that casts the first shadow. No sooner are the young hopefuls lined up before the altar, watched in a markedly predatory manner by all their nearest and dearest, than they are bluntly informed that the way in which they have been passing the time is nothing more nor less than 'coupling like brute beasts that have no understanding'. Then, in the most threatening tones, the Prayer

44

Book proceeds to inform them that the manner in which they intend
to pass the remainder of their time has nothing to do with *them*
whatsoever. It is solely to ensure the procreation of children, or to
avoid sin so that such persons as have not the gift of continency
(who has, my dear sir, who has?) can have their hoggins without
disobeying the seventh commandment or frightening the horses.

After this introduction not even the thrill of paying a mortgage,
or the ecstasy of interminable sleepless nights while some offspring
cuts a tooth, can ever quite dispell an awful feeling of *duty*.

The femmies get so hot under the bra-strap about marriage that
it's only fair to give them the field first. Immediately a Californian
lady (sun-kissed, perhaps, but no maid, since in her own words she
has 'two female children'. Does she mean daughters?) called Judy
Syfers springs to our attention. Mrs Syfers is a wife, or perhaps I
should say a spouse person. She doesn't like it, and to express her
discontent she wrote a short article entitled 'Why I Want a Wife'.
In this she set out in sarcastic vein to list all the advantages of having
a wife, intending thereby to underline the disadvantages of *being* a
wife. She starts:

I belong to that classification of people known as wives.

Elaborately put, you may think. But Judy baby is not giving up.
She has another stab, and this time gets it right:

I am A Wife.

No, I am not just shooting sitting birds for the fun of it. Judy has a
special part to play in our drama. She starts to list what she would
want in a wife. Someone to take care of the children; someone to
cook and wash and mend—suddenly:

I want a wife who is a good nurturant attendant . . .

There! In two balanced, concise words—a whole new life for women! So fast is the English language evolving in California that I had to look up both these words to make sure of the implications of this phrase. They are cosmic. The *Shorter Oxford English Dictionary*, with typically insular backwardness, does not give nurturant, stopping short at one example of 'nurtural'. But we may assume it to derive from nurture. Lacking P. G. Wodehouse's skill in making dictionary quotations come to life, I will say only that nurture covers just about everything from raising lettuces to holding a teaching fellowship. As for attendant, at once two figures come to mind: Fred, who polishes the brasswork and renews defaced VD notices; and a svelte figure in knee breeches who ushers you from ante room to throne room and back. A nurturant attendant, therefore, could be almost anyone in almost any walk of life. No more are you wives, mothers, nurses, au pair girls, teachers—you are nurturant attendants.

No amount of attentive nurturing will reconcile the femmies to marriage. It is difficult to see quite why, because in marriage, as in sex, they wield their greatest power. But marriage, like the proscribed postures in sex, is symbolic of male dominance—and not only of male dominance.

> The wedding is the chief ceremony of the middle-class mythology, and it functions as the official entrée of the spouses to their middle-class status.

Well, Germ old sport, how the old class has changed, or perhaps things are different down under. As an unrepentant, if not fully paid up, member of the middle class I am here to say that my membership depends not on my being married, but on an extraordinary mode of speech very painfully acquired.

Be that as it may, Germaine Greer elaborates another feature of marriage utterly repellent to the modern femmy—it's bourgeois. At least it's not. That is, they don't seem able to decide. Eventually they arrive at the conclusion that it's bourgeois in essence, but has been regrettably copied by a working class aping what it mistakenly believes to be its betters. Have you noticed how radicals despise the supposed beneficiaries of their radicalism? Why shouldn't the working classes have thought of marriage all by themselves?

In addition to symbolic objections to marriage, the femmies list innumerable practical objections to it. Here they are on stronger ground. The woman's career must take second place if the woman wants children. Housework is repetitive and boring, and, worst of all, unpaid. It's lonely at home.

Two considerations arise from this. If the femmies' proposal that housework should be paid is ever adopted, the problem will be quickly solved. Marriage would very shortly cease to exist. As will be seen, men have always been intensely resentful of marriage, and sometimes of their wives. If they had to pay for it as well, no one would ever walk up that aisle.

The second point takes a great deal of courage to state. I shall probably be lynched, but state it I must. *In the absence of children* housework is a soft option. It is certainly boring, but then so are most forms of work. It is not hard work; it leaves plenty of free time, and it is one of the few forms of work that does not have to attain a consistent standard. If you don't feel like polishing the table, give it a quick wipe and leave it till next week. After the arrival of even one child this state of affairs changes dramatically, but it's not a change many women anticipate. To any previously unmarried girl between seventeen and twenty-five, earning her own living, marriage to a man older than herself, and earning much more, is a cop out, a meal ticket. She may love him to distraction; it may subsequently go disastrously wrong for her; but at the moment she does it, on one level anyway, she is thinking, 'This man means to me a house, leisure, no more office hours, free rations'. Of course it's an illusion, or quickly becomes one, but what young person offered a house and a modest private income would turn it down? In their dislike of marriage the femmies miss the element of self-interest that motivates many young women, and until they accept it they won't understand why their own sex doesn't do as they, the femmies, tell it to. And to fail to do what a radical tells you is very, very naughty.

Before we turn to the men, let us follow the couple we last saw gasping at the parson's harsh words from the altar. We will assume that she is only a very mild femmy, and that he is a half-emancipated man, intermittently chauvinistic, but with strong tuggings back to thralldom. In other words a thoroughly boring pair who might well be expected to get on together. They will soon discover, as A. P. Herbert acutely observed:

The critical period in matrimony is breakfast time.

At breakfast woman the wife, woman the nuisance, distant reminders of mother thralldom and sister harassment, and very recent reminders of sexual thralldom, all come together to create an atmosphere of unique unease. The only thing I can say about breakfast is skip it. To start with its very preparation may be delayed by too active attempts to fall into sexual thralldom. Next, woman the nuisance, in her little-woman role, will produce the fried egg with the broken yolk, than which nothing is more infuriating. Hot on the heels of this, woman the nuisance in her blue-stocking guise will interrupt attempts on the crossword with in-the-know comments on the theatre reviews—interruptions all the more unbearable for being secretly welcome as a relief from the obduracy of 3 across. Female caprice will now produce a cup of hot, brown liquid, announced as tea, which turns out to be coffee. It is very upsetting. Our imagined couple will do well to miss breakfast, if only so that they can go through the whole routine, with different props, at dinner. Getting your own breakfast doesn't work, as this is interpreted as an affront.

The true male chauvinist's solution to the breakfast problem is to throw it around the room. Let us therefore desert our newly-wed male, and join the monarchs of the glen, tossing their antlers, tearing at the ground with impassioned forefeet, and roaring from valley to valley, not threats to each other but complaints about their hinds, and the hell of being cooped up in the same forest as them.

Taking numbers into account, I should think more mental suffering had been undergone in the streets leading from St George's, Hanover Square, than in the condemned cells at Newgate.

So wrote Samuel Butler, though his authority is suspect, having himself inclined, so to speak, so far the other way. There are plenty of others, however, to testify that remorse sets in almost straight away. Notice how the hanging motif is returning. It seems no sooner is a man's mind directed to the imminent prospect of marriage than it starts to dwell on hanging. Shakespeare, in *Twelfth Night*, actually offers it as a preferable alternative:

Many a good hanging prevents a bad marriage.

More often it is just a gloomy obsession with capital punishment.

It is a maxim that man and wife should never have it in their power to hang one another.

wrote George Farquhar, hinting that given the opportunity they could hardly be restrained. And again, in *The Recruiting Officer*

Hanging and marriage, you know, go by Destiny.

Male comments on marriage throb with references to judicial death, ineluctable fate, and prison.

> Those who talk most about the blessings of marriage and the constancy of its vows are the very people who declare that if the chain were broken and the prisoner left free to choose, the whole social fabric would fly asunder. You cannot have the argument both ways. If the prisoner is happy, why lock him in? If he is not, why pretend that he is?

Bernard Shaw, posing an unanswerable conundrum. He seems himself to favour the view that if the bonds were released the social order would not fall apart, and in so far as they have been released since he died, and marriage continues to be a widespread habit, history has proved him right. Perhaps the prisoner is not as unhappy as he makes out.

Super-heavyweight male chauvinists have tried to turn marriage to their advantage; to convert it into an arena in which they can throw their weight about, dominate, get their own way, and generally tyrannise all around them. John Milton, who, sad to relate, must be in the running for world champion super-heavyweight male chauvinist of all time, records in *Samson Agonistes*:

> Therefore God's universal law
> Gave to the man despotic power
> Over his female in due awe.

. . . a precept which he tried to apply to his own life. He succeeded to a remarkable extent, being so unbearable that his first wife left him after only six weeks. After three years she was prevailed upon to return and bravely endured Milton's attempts to father a son—resulting in three daughters. She died, of course, and subsequently he undertook two further marriages. Even his blindness did not prevent his putting it over his household in the most despotic manner. Allowing that Robert Graves' account is slightly coloured, Milton's treatment of his first wife still wins several prizes. Not everyone is so fortunate.

I left the room with silent dignity, but caught my foot in the mat.

Charles Pooter would be the archetype of the fully subject male, were it not for his total and magnificent inability to recognise his abject condition. The mat might well have been specially arranged by the dreadful Carrie, but her husband was irrepressible, and for that reason deserves a place among fictional male chauvinists. His action in painting the maid's washstand and bath red was clearly an outbreak of repressed male dominance. Symbols of blood and slaughter, echoes of brides in the bath—all are easily identified by the student of psychological truth.

Those who attain full male chauvinism early enough develop a strong resistance to matrimony. Strangely enough we find John Keats, in spite of his love for Fanny Brawne, coming across almost as strongly as Lord Chesterfield on this point.

The opinion I have of the generality of women—who appear to me as children to whom I would rather give a sugar plum than my time—forms a barrier against matrimony which I rejoice in.

Others reach anti-marriage through experience.

When you're a married man, Samivel, you'll understand a good many things as you don't understand now; but vether it's worth while goin' through so much to learn so little, as the charity boy said ven he got to the end of the alphabet, is a matter o' taste.

So says Mr Weller, perhaps the greatest marriage-avoidance counsellor in literature. Even Oscar Wilde leaves us the rather barbed comment:

In married life three is company and two none.

The last word on anti-marriage must rest with Robert Louis

Stevenson, not because he is in any way gratifyingly rude about women, but because his remark is a particularly penetrating one.

> Marriage is a step so grave and decisive that it attracts light-headed. variable men by its very awfulness.

He is quite right. There is a sort of dizzy silliness in the way most men approach the altar, and our weighty, profound male chauvinist is not typically associated with holy wedlock.

During the first few years, marriage witnesses the sexual battle at its fiercest. Thereafter most couples abandon the fray through sheer exhaustion, and the victory, in so far as home life is usually maintained, is the woman's. It is something of a pyrrhic victory however, since most women, once they have got what they wanted in the shape of home and children, then decide that it's not what they wanted after all. The confrontation between woman the wife and the male chauvinist is the least pure form of sexual antagonism, complicated as it is by all sorts of personal considerations, but in it the woman wields great power, and it is one of the few areas where the law is on her side. Most reluctantly we must advise aspirants to true chauvinism to avoid matrimony, unless they enter it in the spirit of an ordeal to stoke the fires of anti-feminism.

I have perhaps, been too dismissive of the femmy position on marriage. Since all parties have grounds for complaint, we should listen to any new ideas that may crop up. The 'stem' family (looking after auntie) is put forward as an alternative to the nuclear family (mum and dad and junior all in the same flat). A huge country house full of all the loved ones and some unrelated friends as well sounds a great idea, and Germaine Greer expounds on it at some length. She describes the stem family at work in an Italian village, and toys with the idea of settling with friends in a large Italian house in a commune of truly shared responsibility and equal relationships. Then comes the crunch.

The house and garden would be worked by a local family who lived in the house.

Aha! Paid, I hope.

So it seems that there is no solution. But wait! I am ignoring something. What do I hear wafting across the pole from the distant strands of sunny California? The forlorn piping of a lone femmy? We have forgotten Judy. She points the way. In the future we shall not marry. We shan't even live together. We will sign mutually agreed contracts outlining the fair division of the onerous but rewarding tasks and responsibilities of . . .

nurturant attendants.

5

WOMAN THE OPPONENT
or the on-going sexist dialectic

We have followed our male chauvinist through his encounters with
women in their four most serious manifestations. We have seen that
only a few favoured specimens break through to full chauvinism.
We have seen how the troops of thralldom prowl and prowl around
encompassing the downfall of all but the most resilient. And we
have seen, on the flanks of the main armies, the astute guerrilla
tactics of the femmies as they snipe away at the male position. It is
now time to look into some of the odder aspects of male chauvinism,
and also to the future which, I must say in advance, is bleak indeed.

> The education of women should always be relative to that of men. To
> please, to be useful to us, to make us love and esteem them, to educate
> us when young, to take care of us when grown up, to advise, to console
> us, to render our lives easy and agreeable. These are the duties of women
> at all times, and what they should be taught in their infancy.

Who is this? This man of reason, sound-bottomed? You're not
going to believe it. Weedy old J.-J. Rousseau—in other respects the
fount and origin of all the silly-season liberal ills that beset us—he
and none other penned these admirable words. It just goes to show
that you never know where Nicolas Chauvin will rear his head next.
To find J.-J. in such exalted company as that of Dr Johnson is

strange indeed, but he was an unstable, erratic creature, and perhaps this was merely a flash in the pan. He cannot be said to have reached a high standard of chauvinism, and I would now like to contrast a fictional character who seems to me to have attained a degree of male chauvinism so subtle and highly developed as to be unique.

> Slowly and solemnly he was borne into Briony Lodge, and laid out in the principal room, while I still observed the proceedings from my post by the window. The lamps had been lit, but the blinds had not been drawn, so that I could see Holmes as he lay on the couch. I do not know whether he was seized with compunction at that moment for the part he was playing, but I know that I never felt more heartily ashamed of myself in my life than when I saw the beautiful creature against whom I was conspiring, or the grace and kindliness with which she waited upon the injured man. And yet it would be the blackest treachery to Holmes to draw back now from the part which he had entrusted to me. I hardened my heart and took the smoke rocket from under my ulster. After all, I thought, we are not injuring her. We are but preventing her from injuring another . . . at the signal I tossed my rocket into the room with a cry of 'Fire'.

I make no apology for the length of this extract. It is worth it if only for the picture of two such certifiable lunatics capering about the metropolis bunging bombs into boudoirs. However, Dr Watson's attitudes and musings are a study. The story, as all afficionados will know, is *A Scandal in Bohemia*, and the woman is The Woman, Irene Adler. Watson does not dwell on the fact that the whole venture is illegal, but then that is not particularly surprising since the response of these two Baker Street bandits to the law was always what the moderns would call flexible. He does, however, dimly perceive that he is badly in the wrong in an ethical sense, and close attention must be paid to Dr Watson's ethical sense since, although woolly, it was extremely highly developed. Loyalty to Holmes, however, comes first, so it is not surprising to see him choke back his misgivings.

What is wonderful is the magnificent detachment that Watson achieves, and it is this that marks him down as such a well developed male chauvinist. He is so emancipated from thralldom that he can wallow in the most abject sentiment. The first part of this extract, taken out of context, might be a prime example of male subjectivism. But, on the real Watson, it has not the slightest effect. He still, with the utmost cheerfulness, throws a smoke bomb into the lady's room (where spirit lamps are burning!) to enable Holmes to locate her private correspondence with a view to stealing it later. His own wife, after her initial introduction, becomes such a shadowy figure as to be almost invisible. Holmes has only to appear in some unlikely disguise and whisper, 'The game's afoot, Watson!', for the doctor to drop both wife and medical practice with hardly a word and shove off with Holmes on some totally irresponsible escapade. Do not be fooled by Watson's superficial soft-heartedness with women. It serves as a foil to Holmes' supposedly chilly severity with them. Beneath the surface it is a very different matter. Holmes, at least once or twice, is seriously affected by the women they encounter. Watson, for all his gushings, remains footloose and fancy free in the most frivolous way.

It is an enviable approach to women, of such rarity that it deserves a name all of its own. We shall designate it 'condescensional solipsism'.

Of all masculine techniques the femmies hate condescensional solipsism the most. It is impervious to nearly all their attacks. A good condescensional solipsist could actually *join the feminist movement* without losing his male chauvinist status. And the femmies would know it, too. There are very few true examples of condescensional solipsists. I know a monk, an ordained priest, whose job is that of pastor and confessor to a mountain-top convent of nuns. As the only man in a female community of some hundreds, who has taken vows of celibacy and whose normal career would have been spent in exclusively masculine company, he has to be described as someone who has beaten the system, but the peculiar circumstances of his order and calling deny him full CS status. Uriah Heep might be on our list, but he went too far. Perhaps the Amazon menfolk perfected CS. We shall never know. So far as I can see, Dr Watson MD stands alone, as any man who can sigh gustily about a beautiful, graceful, kind creature and then throw a bomb at her, should do.

Even impure forms of condescensional solipsism are rare. Plenty of examples exist of attitudes to women which are sentimentally favourable on the surface, but by nuance and innuendo satirical and dismissive underneath. These attitudes cannot qualify as CS, because it is their *intention* to attack women. Our true exponent of CS must be genuinely attached to women. He must like them. He must not overtly patronise them. But he must keep in reserve, in the core of his being, the freedom to throw bombs at them whenever circumstances so dictate. One ambiguous example highlights the difficulties of CS.

> But there's wisdom in women, of more than they have known,
> And thoughts go blowing through them, are wiser than their own.

It is impossible to decide whether Rupert Brooke is here well on the way to chronic, multiple male subjectivism, or whether he intends the belittling implications of these lines. It could be just another woman-on-a-pedestal-vehicle-of-intuitive-wisdom eulogy. On the other hand the suggestion that women are empty vessels, mere transmitters of some ether-borne source of knowledge, is highly offensive—to women. Only the greatest condescensional solipsists can combine genuine grovelling with genuine ascendancy.

We mustn't overlook Browning, who brought off a considerable feat. This brave man tackled a blue-stocking, and not just any blue-stocking, but one of the most formidable femmies of his age or any other, from a position of near condescensional solipsism with a very interesting twist to it. He wrote of George Sand:

Thou large-brained woman and large-hearted man.

Why did he put it that way round? A straightforward chauvinist would have attributed head to man and heart to woman. But Browning had worked out an ingenious method of wounding the good lady French novelist. It was, after all, quite a feat to publish novels attacking marriage in the 1830s, even if she did take refuge in a male pseudonym. Her later works all testify to the regard in which she held Intellect. Browning, in attributing intellect to the female side of her personality, makes the insinuation that intellect is something trivial, nit-picking, something for women. Large-heartedness, however, is all male. No more subtle or concise way of displaying male arrogance in an otherwise faultlessly generous tribute could have been devised.

These are great heights, and have been scaled by few. Nor does it seem likely that they will be scaled very often in the future. We must, I think, accept that the femmies are going to win. The twentieth century is the age of the guerrilla. Regular forces cannot stand against him; they are too costly and unwieldy to deploy. Their organisation creaks with age; they are governed by attitudes slow to adapt. The more insane the ideology with which the guerrilla is armed, the more successful he is likely to be. The femmies are guerrillas par excellence. There is nowhere they cannot infiltrate. No target is secure from a sudden hit-and-run attack. As the people are to the guerrilla, a base, a source of supplies and recruits, and camouflage in which he can hide, so is the family to the femmy. The days of male chauvinism are numbered, and since this is so perhaps we had better take a look at what the femmies have in store for us.

> In its most general formulation the goal of the radical feminist movement is the complete elimination of the sex-role system.

Thus Anna Koedt, Ellen Levine, and Anita Rapone, a triad of transatlantic femmies, announce their aims. You may well wonder what the sex-role system is, and what its elimination entails. I've got very bad news for all of you. According to Kate Millett its elimination will mean:

> The attainment . . . of both sexes to viable humanity.

Your present humanity is totally unviable. Go back and change it. Along the road to viable humanity we shall shed such useless encumbrances as separatist character-structure, the male supremacist ethic, and enforced perverse heterosexuality. What would we do without the intelligentsia? Give something a name, however hideous, and then you can eliminate it! If Millett, Koedt, Levine and Rapone hadn't come along and identified all these things we might have gone on happily committing them, unaware of the frightful error we had fallen into. I am particularly worried about enforced perverse heterosexuality. Is it venial or mortal? Should I see my analyst?

The millennium will also bring with it:

> The end of sexuality in the forms in which it has existed historically—brutality, violence, capitalism, exploitation, and warfare—that it may cease to be hatred and become love.

You, callow and uninstructed male chauvinist pig that you are, thought that brutality, violence and warfare were caused by aggression, and that capitalism and exploitation were caused by greed and insensitivity. You were quite wrong. Anyone versed in psychological truth could have told you—they are all caused by rampant sexuality. And the collapse of all the fighting and grabbing that used to characterise sex will usher in the new age of:

> Bisex . . . so that the sex act ceases to be arbitrarily polarised into male and female, to the exclusion of sexual expression between members of the same sex.

Calling it the sex act does make it sound so very *functional*, and who's doing the excluding, for heaven's sake? And in view of the importance of the biological functions involved, it's a bit curious to describe the dear old sex act as 'arbitrarily polarised'. I think Millett foresees a golden future where everyone will make love to everyone irrespective of age, sex, colour, attractiveness or the need to reproduce. Reports reaching me from Surbiton suggest that such practices are already widespread, but I find it difficult to believe. Remove the element of mutual attraction and you really are left with a mere function. The femmy heaven is beginning to sound very tedious.

Most of the femmy proposals are either silly or boring, but one is downright sinister, and in making it Kate Millett allows the despotism implicit in so many radical ideas to peep through. She calls for:

> The end of the ancient oppression of the young under the patriarchal proprietary family, their chattel status, the attainment of human rights presently denied them, *the professionalisation and therefore improvement of their care* . . . [my italics]

The parents' relationship with their children is loaded with pejorative words: oppression, patriarchal, proprietary, chattel, denial of rights—a rather wild view of parenthood however much you favour extending the law to give children greater protection. But the alternative is so beautifully stated: 'professionalisation' and therefore improvement! Of course! Of course! Train people and give them degrees, and of course it's better for them to bring up others' children! That may be la Millett's idea, but to me it sounds like state baby farms.

The female love of sway is given full rein in the manifesto of The Feminists, a New York group we have already met in Chapter 1. Nominally opposed to elitism, it nonetheless lays down such stringent membership terms that the group has no alternative but to become an elite. Hotly opposed to marriage it lays down a quota of married women in the membership which may not be exceeded. Clearly married women are seen as dangerous deviationists who might vote against pure feminism. Tasks within the group are shared out by what the manifesto describes as 'lot'. It does not make clear whether this involves a process of voting, or whether it is entirely haphazard. It does make clear that the tasks cannot be declined and that expulsion will result from inadequate attendance at meetings. And these are not the only grounds for getting the boot:

> A single action which goes against the will of the group, constitutes an exploitation of the group, or seriously endangers its work or survival, is grounds for expulsion.

The will of the group, forsooth. You can't have it spelt out much clearer than that—no individuals here! Without quoting at length from their clouds of opaque prose, I cannot give the reader a sample of the depressing atmosphere created by The Feminists. They exude small-minded fanaticism of the type that I imagine to have held sway in pre-revolutionary Bolshevik circles. Exclusive groups of this kind feed on themselves and grow vast, so to speak, on nothing. Their vocabulary becomes more and more top-heavy as they seek out new ways of saying the same old things, and with this vocabulary they build huge structures of what in an earlier chapter we learned to call MT. When they get a chance to foist their MT on the world, the results are predictably horrible. I cannot resist one more example of unrivalled MT, from Anna Koedt again:

> It remains for us women to fully develop a new dialectic of sex class— an analysis of the way in which sexual identity and institutions reinforce one another.

Roll on, desexualisation.

It almost makes me think with longing of J.-J. Rousseau, and anything that can do that *must* be bad.

The male chauvinist pig still roams at large on his ancestral grazing grounds, but, poor dumb anachronistic creature, he is doomed. Femmies on foot will stalk him through the tangled forest. When he breaks for the open, mounted, pig-sticking femmies will ride him down. In the night he will fall into pits dug for him by vindictive femmies, or be hoisted suddenly tree top-wards by some cunningly devised spring. Grunting and squealing and clattering his tusks he will from time to time turn to charge his tormentors, but the roar and flash of some fearless femmy's express will bowl him over before he has a chance to roll the whites of his eyes. Photographed in triumphal posture over heaps of dead pigs, the femmies will meet, let us say on the 'conceptual analysis committee' of their group, and boast of the tusks they have mounted on their walls.

Hunting will be augmented by the destruction of his habitat in femmy interests. The grazing and the forests will disappear. The Athenaeum will become a crèche for the babies of battered-un-married-mother activists. Lords will be given over to lacrosse. From cover to cover, in ever dwindling numbers, the last male chauvinist pigs will scurry until the lineal descendants of Samuel Johnson,

Lord Chesterfield, Lord Byron, Lord Tennyson and Bluebeard the Pirate are no more.

Perhaps in some remote vestigial forest, the last male chauvinist pigs will be given a refuge. Safari-carloads of repentant femmies will come to photograph this magnificent animal, so nearly and tragically hunted to extinction. There in the peaceful shade of the great trees he will tear imperiously at the ground with his tusks; acquisitively grab the best truffle; sneer at his sows; shoulder them out of the way, and generally keep the feeble flame of civilisation alight through the dark ages.

Perhaps it will not come to this. After all, in the words of Aristotle:

> The female is a female by virtue of a certain *lack* of qualities; we should regard the female nature as afflicted with a natural defectiveness.

If this is so, and if men have been right in assuming women's intrinsic inferiority, perhaps the femmies will simply fail to do anything at all. One does not have to read very far into femmy literature to discover at least one natural defect that Aristotle may have had in mind. In doing so, the reader will be delighted to hear, I have unearthed the 'function-activity theory' (remember the F-AT?—if not, see Chapter 1) and am now able to offer an exposition of this, the most majestic and subtle intellectual concept yet to sprout from the seed-bed of femmy philosophy

> Our present theory, the Function-Activity Theory, relates oppression and power by defining oppression in terms of confinement to inherently powerless activities.

Well, I must say, this comes as something of a disappointment. I had hoped that function-activity might turn out to be the elaboration of a new, exciting and, of course, utterly liberating sex posture —perhaps the man strapped to a trampoline with the woman jumping on to him—but it turns out to be a mere 'adjustment' of the meaning of oppression. I could quote at length from the 'conceptual analysis' which follows this statement (in which the words 'definition' and 'elimination' are constantly reiterated; you 'define' something, that is you invent it, and then you 'eliminate' it, that is you set about harassing your predetermined enemy armed with this wholly arbitrary theory) but I think the defect I mentioned is obvious. It is the total absence of common sense and humour.

One more, please, just one more

> We need a new premise for society: that the most basic right of every individual is to create the terms of its [sic] own definition.

All else confusion indeed.